# These are my friends

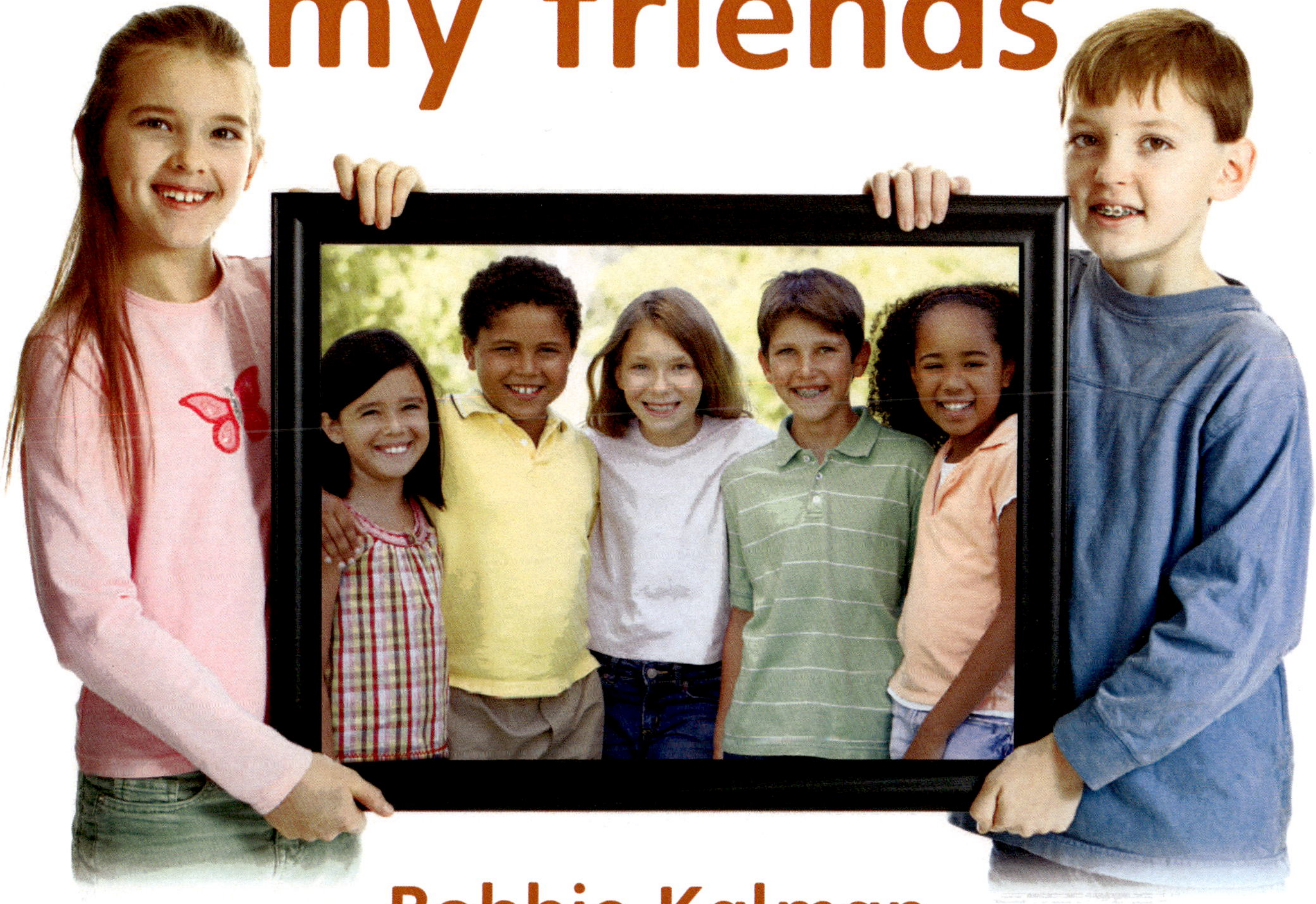

Bobbie Kalman

Crabtree Publishing

crabtreebooks.com

# Created by Bobbie Kalman

## Crabtree Publishing

**crabtreebooks.com 800-387-7650**



In Canada: We acknowledge the financial support of the Government of Canada through the Canada Book Fund for our publishing activities.

Hardcover 978-0-7787-9439-4
Paperback 978-0-7787-9483-7
Ebook (pdf) 978-0-7787-9203-1

Printed in Canada/072024/CP20240710

**Library and Archives Canada Cataloguing in Publication**

Kalman, Bobbie, 1947-
These are my friends / Bobbie Kalman.

(My world)
ISBN 978-0-7787-9439-4 (bound).--
ISBN 978-0-7787-9483-7 (pbk.)

1. Friendship--Juvenile literature. I. Title. II. Series: My world (St. Catharines, Ont.)

BF723.F68K34 2010 j158.2'5 C2009-906098-1

**Published in Canada**
**Crabtree Publishing**
616 Welland Avenue
St. Catharines, Ontario
L2M 5V6

**Published in the United States**
**Crabtree Publishing**
347 Fifth Avenue
Suite 1402-145
New York, NY 10016

Author and Editor-in-Chief: Bobbie Kalman
Educational consultants: Reagan Miller, Joan King
Editors: Enlynne Paterson, Joan King, Kathy Middleton
Proofreader: Crystal Sikkens
Design: Bobbie Kalman, Katherine Kantor
Photo research: Bobbie Kalman
Production coordinator: Katherine Kantor
Prepress technician: Katherine Kantor

Photographs: iStockphoto: p. 15
All other photographs by Shutterstock

**Library of Congress Cataloging-in-Publication Data**

Kalman, Bobbie.
These are my friends / Bobbie Kalman.
p. cm. -- (My world)
ISBN 978-0-7787-9483-7 (pbk. : alk. paper) --
ISBN 978-0-7787-9439-4 (reinforced library binding : alk. paper)
1. riendship in children--Juvenile literature. 2. Friendship--Juvenile literature. I. Title. II. Series.

BF723.F68K35 2010
177'.62--dc22

2009041214

# Words to know

best friend

brothers and sisters

group hug

music friends

pet friend

team

These are my friends.
I have old friends and new friends.
I have good friends and best friends.
I love having friends!

These are my friends.
They go to my school.
They live near my home.
We meet at the pool.
We go to the playground, too.
There are many things we like to do.

Sometimes we read a book.
Sometimes we take a walk.
Sometimes we ride our bikes.
Sometimes we sit and talk.

There are many things
my friends and I share.
We share group hugs
to show that we care.

These are my friends.
They are my sisters and brothers.
I have six friends to play with,
not counting the others!

Do you have pet friends?
Do they love you?
Do they cheer you up,
when you are feeling blue?

"Ha, ha! Is it true?"

These are my music friends.
We sing, dance, and play.
We like music so much,
we could play all day!

We sing and rock,
around the clock.

My friends and I
are part of a team.
When we won the game,
it felt like a dream!

What are your dreams?
Will they come true?
Do you share them with friends?
Do they share theirs with you?

My friends make me happy.
My friends listen, too.
My friends make me smile.
My friends are you!

These are
my friends.

Did I know
from the start,
that each of my
friends would become
part of my heart?

# Notes for adults

## What is a friend?

Human beings are social animals that need friends. This book talks about friends in a rhyming poem and looks at what kinds of friends children have, such as school friends, pet friends, sibling friends, musical friends, and teammates.

## Exploration of friendship

Ask the children how they met their friends and what they look for in a friend. Do they have a best friend, do they have sibling friends or pet friends, or are they friends with many people? What do they need to do to keep their friends? Explore the following topics with them:

- sharing and cooperation
- generosity and kindness
- resolving conflicts
- rules of play
- saying "no" to dangerous play and to hurting others

## Letters to friends

Ask each child to write a poem to a friend. The children should not put their names on the poems. After the poems are written, they will put them into blank envelopes. All the envelopes will be put into a box and mixed up. Each child will then select an envelope and read the enclosed poem "from a friend." After everyone has read a poem, ask the children how the poems made them feel. The children could then have the option of keeping their poems or posting them on the bulletin board.